THE PROBLEMS OF POLITICAL APPOINTEES IN FEDERAL GOVERNMENT:

CAUSES, EFFECTS, AND SOLUTIONS

MATTHEW HOWARD

2017

The Problems of Political Appointees in Federal Government: Causes, Effects, and Solutions.

Print ISBN: 979-8-55-965455-3
Kindle ASIN: B01N7VEXYM

Educational Series, Volume Five.
2020 Paperback Edition.

Contents

Author's Note

This work was originally a literature review completed for my graduate coursework in Public Administration in December 2016.

Articles found only online or in other non-paginated reproductions of the original text are cited in the text as (Author, Year) without a page number. Page numbers of the original printed text, where verified, are shown in the *References* section.

I. Introduction: Significance.

What are the effects of the short terms served by politically appointed leaders in the federal government? The literature relevant to this question reveals that short-term service is only part of the problem with political appointees, and that the downsides of the short terms are inextricably linked to other undesirable results of the appointee system. A simple solution such as extending the terms to greater lengths would potentially reduce the negative results of short-term service, but not address certain fundamental flaws in the system. Therefore, this literature review will address the totality of the negative results and the recent research into them—a broader scope than the original question, but one granting an important perspective on the matter, and the elements of its solution.

To be fair, political appointees do more than present problems. They are often valuable assets whose contribution to governmental operations should be acknowledged before we critically examine their shortcomings and negative effects. In government, no fine line exists between administration and politics. The two are tightly woven together, much more so than in the private sector where many workers can simply "get the job done" without worrying too much about political maneuvering. In the politically charged reality of the federal government, appointees bring valuable "political experience, ties to the President, and familiarity with the news media and key stakeholders" (Woodrow, 2013). And, compared to career executives and administrators, they "also tend to have more education and a longer history in private or non-profit management", albeit *outside* the civil service which now calls on them for duty (ibid).

Yet for all their value, political appointees have negative effects on their coworkers, on our government's ability to serve the public effectively, and even on international relations. These problems are caused by the short duration of their appointments, the earning of these appointments as favors to campaign workers and party members rather than skilled administrators who make careers out of civil service, and the detrimental effects this political-based leadership exerts on the careerists who struggle to carry out agency missions. The literature resoundingly agrees that these negative outcomes of the political appointee system exist, and that they pose a significant threat to public administration.

A. Size. The question is significant to the study

of leadership because, first of all, it encompasses the massive bureaucracy of the entire federal government, and the ever-growing thousands of political appointees in its top echelons. The United States, compared to other nations, has one of the highest numbers of political appointees in the world. "Gallo and Lewis point out that 'the United States has significantly more political appointments than other developed democracies'", with anywhere from 3,000–4,000 appointments in "policy or confidential positions" which depend on the White House's involvement (Woodrow, 2013). This number has increased steadily over the past forty years (Kettl, 2012, p. 287).

But that number is far from the complete picture of executive branch appointments, which we will clarify in greater detail in the *Relevant Terminology* section. All told, the executive branch has more than 9,000 positions filled by appointments. Appointees, whether political or otherwise, make up a significant segment of the executive branch—a segment which exists at the top layers of agency management and leadership hierarchies. The problem is more than a human resources concern about staffing. It concerns the uppermost layers of executive branch leaders tasked with providing leadership to departments, programs, and agencies created to serve the public by implementing far-reaching federal policy.

B. Morale and Performance. From an organizational leadership perspective, the question addresses significant effects on the morale of federal workers and agencies, and the resulting decline in performance which accompanies it. That political appointees are "often underqualified" and hired from outside the administrative system "has a demoralizing effect on ambitious career professionals, depriving them of incentives to excel" (Woodrow, 2013). A dispirited and de-incentivized cadre of administrative professionals in the federal government can only have negative effects on governmental performance and the delivery of quality service to the American public.

When career professionals leave their positions in frustration, as happened in large numbers at FEMA from 2001–2003 under Director Joe Allbaugh, they take "institutional memory and critical skills with them" (ibid). (Allbaugh's appointment followed his management of Bush's campaign.) This theme pervades the literature: When federal workers retire out of frustration with the lack of oversight of political appointees, it leaves government agencies at risk of being unable to protect the public—the people and interests they exist to support. Institutional memory, skills, and experience vanish, and those who are left behind must carry on with less support and guidance.

The effects of political appointees on morale, effectiveness, and retirement rates among career executives and administrators will be explored in greater detail with specific examples in the *Historical Background* section.

C. Accountability. *The Federal Yellow Book* lists "every management position in the five departmental leadership 'compartments' headed by Senate-confirmed presidential appointees" in the various cabinets (Light, 2004). These positions include an ever-thickening layer of deputy secretaries, undersecretaries, assistant secretaries, chiefs of staff to secretaries, associate deputy secretaries, and deputy assistant secretaries—and the number of these titles grows each year.

"Roughly half of the executive titles involve career appointments, while the other half involve political appointments not subject to Senate confirmation" (ibid). The differences between these two categories of appointments will be explored in more detail in the *Relevant Terminology* section. Together, they make up "fifty-two potential managerial layers... from top to bottom in the federal government" (Kettl, 2012, p. 288).

The literature expresses resounding agreement that "the increasing layers of political appointees mean that there are fewer career executives who have the requisite experience to serve effectively at the highest levels of departments and agencies" (Pfiffner, 2012, p. 38). With leaders chosen for political reasons rather than skill, merit, or proven performance, careerists get fewer opportunities to advance through these layers into the top ranks of leadership and develop experience at that level. But the problem goes beyond performance and job qualifications. The political appointee system and its deep layering also create a complex hierarchy in which accountability is difficult to come by.

Paul Light, who studies the federal bureaucracy for the Brookings Institution, concludes this thickening of government with political appointees has an "obvious" effect on "public confidence" because it erodes accountability (Light, 2004). With an endless roster of secretaries and deputies, who exactly is held responsible for malfeasances, incompetence, and poor performance? No one knows for sure, and the general public perceives the effect both as government's incompetence and its tendency to serve itself rather than the people.

"No one is ever held accountable for government performance because no one *can* be held accountable," says Light, and this is due not only to the complexity of the hierarchy but to the way "vacancies anywhere in the chain of command can produce long delays in the movement of information and guidance" (Light, 2004). In other words, the hierarchy is both complex and full of empty offices. One of the more egregious examples comes from the 1980s. At the beginning of Ronald Reagan's *second* term in the Oval Office, in 1986, "one-sixth of the 176 cabinet department positions that required presidential nomination and Senate confirmation were either vacant or occupied by persons as only 'acting' in their position" (Kettl, 2012, p. 294). And that was just in the cabinet.

The 1998 *Vacancies Reform Act* attempted to curtail this phenomenon by imposing limits on how long positions could be filled by "acting" administrators, but agencies merely responded by being slow to report the vacancies—or simply never reporting them at all (ibid). It is small wonder the American people do not know who to hold accountable when it looks like no one is there.

The source of these vacancies is typically the process by which executive branch nominees must be reviewed and confirmed by the Senate, a problematic process which contributes to the numerous staffing problems the federal system faces. As of 2012, the average time for an appointee to receive confirmation was ten months, more than triple the average confirmation time of three months in the 1960s (Pfiffner, 2012, p. 37).

This delay creates both a reduction in human resources available to agencies and an increase in turnover in managerial positions (Mendelson, 2015, p. 1571). "Management positions filled by appointees show systematically higher rates of turnover on average than positions filled by careerists", and this labor cost, hidden in the appointee system, is a significant one for the federal system (Pfiffner, 2012, p. 39). The *Historical Background* section will address the negative effects of high turnover in greater detail.

The positions left vacant while the Senate muddles through its procedures may also slow down the executive branch's regulatory review (Mendelson, 2015, p. 1572). This is the process by which the White House reviews the policy decisions of executive branch agencies (ibid, p. 1587). To be fair, the Senate is not entirely to blame for delays, as the executive branch's nomination process which precedes it is also a major source of delay (Pfiffner, 2012, p. 39). Neither does all the blame fall on the President's shoulders. With so many appointee positions to fill, a President typically focuses his personal attention on choosing his cabinet members and has comparatively little attention to devote to finding the thousands of appointees below the cabinet level (Kettl, 2012, p. 290).

D. International Scope. Appointees do not only affect domestic affairs; their reach is international due to appointments as diplomats and ambassadors. The literature is inconclusive regarding the overall effect. Career administrators and experts do not always rise to the top levels of the diplomatic system as foreign ministers to serve abroad, a statement as true of other nations as it is of the United States. Instead, these positions sometimes go to "people who have made their mark in domestic politics, business, or society, and who may hitherto have evinced very little interest in international affairs. The professionals are passed over in favor of... people who have 'a known political connection or whose selection was motivated by political considerations'" (Lloyd, 2006, p. 1). The percentage of political appointees given ambassadorships under George W. Bush, Bill Clinton, and Richard Nixon is estimated to be thirty percent of all ambassador positions (ibid).

Despite the mandate against considering campaign contributions when making appointments, per the US Foreign Service Act of 1980, "thirty of Bush's 'pioneers' (top fundraisers) or their spouses in the 2000 election were appointed to ambassadorships," including posts in

"London, Paris, other European capitals, and some of the Caribbean islands" (ibid, p. 3). The London ambassadorship, for example, went to William Farish, a "multi-millionaire horse breeder who, with his wife, jointly donated $37,875 to Republican candidates and party committees, $100,000 to the Bush-Cheney inaugural fund, and $5,000 to the 2000 election recount fund. Farish also gave Millie the dog to Bush's father George, the former president, who was one of his tennis partners." (ibid).

While at first glance it appears Farish bought himself an ambassadorship, he was clearly well-connected, and these connections can serve a purpose in political relationships between nations. Put simply, a political appointee knows people, and these contacts are more likely to respond to phone calls and dinner invitations from someone they know, as compared to a relative stranger they have no prior dealings with.

But such appointments come with potential downsides, including public embarrassments caused by appointees who have more money than they do diplomatic skills. As with domestic affairs, these appointments can "have a disheartening effect" on career administrators, "especially if it means they are denied headship of the top posts" (ibid, p. 16). It takes no great feat of imagination to see why a civil servant who has dedicated his entire career to public policy would take offense at serving under a leader whose primary qualification was an elite roster for dinner parties, and whose main field of experience was breeding horses instead of implementing programs to achieve executive branch policy goals.

A paper presented at the 2006 Annual Meeting of the International Studies Association proposed a solution: Place career administrators in deputy positions to ameliorate these downsides and make good use of their skills once relationships are solidified by the appointees.

II. Summary of the Literature.

A. Relevant Terminology: Types and Numbers of Appointees. Not all appointees within the federal system are political ones. For example, the federal government maintains a Senior Executive Service composed of "the elite corps of federal administrators" from which career executives and administrators may be chosen for appointments to key positions (Woodrow, 2013). Appointing careerists from this labor pool is distinctly different from giving appointments to campaign supporters and party members, and other appointments of a purely political nature.

The distinction is no small matter. A study published in *Journal of Public Administration Research and Theory*, April 2012, found a sharp difference in the performance of agencies run by political appointees compared to the appointed career executives. The study used the Bush administration's *Program Assessment Rating Tool* (PART) to evaluate "1,000 federal programs and more than 350 managers—some of whom oversaw multiple programs" (ibid).

Programs run by political appointees who had worked for the national party or the presidential campaign "earned PART scores nine to thirteen points lower than those of programs run by nonpolitical appointees", and programs managed by career executives "with previous agency experience tended to earn better scores even when measured against political appointees with experience in business or the non-profit sector" (ibid). In short, leadership by political appointees produces quantifiably inferior performance results compared to that of career executives.

Robert Goldenkoff, Director of Strategic Issues for the Government Accountability Office (GAO), describes yet another kind of "appointee" to add to our terminology. "Direct hire", a hiring flexibility created by Congress in 2002, "allows an agency to appoint people to positions without adherence to certain competitive examination requirements when there is a severe shortage of qualified candidates or a critical hiring need" (Goldenkoff, 2008, p. 10). This is not a political appointment but a practical solution to a human resources problem: labor shortages and vacant positions. As of 2004, however, agencies were "making limited use of these available flexibilities", a statement supported in more depth by the GAO's report *Human Capital: Increasing Agencies' Use of New Hiring Flexibilities* (ibid).

A 2012 article in *The Public Manager* further clarifies the types and numbers of political appointees working in the federal system. "Each presidential administration is faced with appointing about 3,000" executive branch positions (800 of which require Senate confirmation), plus:

- 3,000 part-time presidential appointments.
- 200–300 U.S. attorneys, marshals, and ambassadors requiring Senate confirmation.
- 700 White House staff appointments.
- 800 non-career Senior Executive Service appointments.
- 1,500 Schedule C (GS-15 and below) appointments (Pfiffner, 2012, p.37).

B. Theories and Concepts.

"Any organization is only as good as its people. Therefore, effective government requires a first-rate workforce. Given the scope and breadth of the federal government—arguably the largest, the most diverse, and the most complex entity on earth—we can afford nothing less than top talent in key government posts."
—Former U.S. Comptroller General David M. Walker, 2007.

Strategic Human Capital Management. Insofar as political appointees comprise a part of the federal labor force, they are studied within the framework of labor and human resources theory. Currently, the most common framework for these theories is what Director Robert Goldenkoff and others call "strategic human capital management." What does it mean to view employees as human capital?

Put simply, "employees are not costs to be avoided or resources to be consumed, but assets to be valued and investments to be strategically managed to maximize their usefulness" (Nathanson, 2005, p. 42). As assets, employees' "value can be enhanced through investments in training, technology, incentives, and other areas" (Walker, 2007). David M. Walker, former U.S. Comptroller General, believes the effectiveness of this way of thinking depends on how well ideas about investing in human capital are aligned with "an organization's mission, core values, vision for the future, specific goals and objectives, and current and expected resource levels" (ibid).

Such language is congruent with current trends in private business. The words "human capital" are fairly new to the federal government's vocabulary, having been introduced in the late 1990s by Comptroller General Walker (Nathanson, 2005, p. 42). Congress and the executive branch have since embraced this terminology and created both assessment tools and positions based on managing their investment in workers.

Federal Assessment Tools. *The President's Management Agenda* (PMA) is a development of the Bush administration which includes an initiative based on strategic human capital management. The Office of Management and Budget (OMB) creates a scorecard each quarter which tracks executive branch agencies' progress in carrying out this initiative. Another tool in the federal toolbox comes from the Bush administration: the *Program Assessment Rating Tool* (PART), "which scores agencies' effectiveness on a scale of one to 100" (Woodrow, 2013).

Furthermore, the *Chief Human Capital Officers Act* of 2002 mandates that every executive agency create a senior official position "whose major role is to think about the workforce strategically" (Nathanson, 2005, p. 43). This position is an appointed one, a fact which may have some bearing on how such an official would view the roles of—and problems created by—appointees.

C. Historical Background. The historical background of political appointees in federal government begins with the nature of our system compared to other countries; specifically, the separation of powers built into our system since the earliest days of our Constitution. Concerned about the abuses of power in the monarchies of

Europe, the authors of the Constitution divided government into three branches: the executive, the legislature, and the judiciary. Here our problems began.

Why Appointees? While the system works well at preventing any one of the branches from assuming totalitarian control, it leaves the President "less in command of administrative agencies" than his European counterparts working under parliamentary systems (Kettl, 2012, p. 287). European systems are often set up so the controlling party of the legislature must match the party of the executive leader. This eliminates a party-against-party struggle that often consumes the energy of the American political system. When Congress exerts control of executive agencies through "oversight and intervention," a Congress controlled by one political party will often be working at odds against the political and policy goals of a President of another party; this contrasts with parliamentary systems where "leaders can count on legislative support because their party or coalition has the most votes" (ibid).

This split in the American system can lead to presidential feelings that agencies are unresponsive to his direction and failing to carry out the policy promises he has made to the American public. Political appointees are a potential solution which establishes agency leadership that is favorable and responsive to a President's wishes, working as a unified coalition with the President instead of being hampered by political differences or congressional interference. But as the next section on *Poor Performance* concludes, this goal of responsiveness becomes irrelevant when an agency is rendered incapable of taking effective action due to the same political appointees the President has staffed there.

Poor Performance. The shortcomings of political appointees often make national headlines when they fail miserably at their jobs. Most well-known to Americans is the poor performance of Michael Brown. Brown ascended from his appointment as general counsel of the Federal Emergency Management Agency (FEMA) to become its Administrator—a title which in this case means its acting head. Brown's lack of experience in handling actual emergencies could hardly have come at a worse time. After Hurricane Katrina hammered the Gulf Coast in August 2005, FEMA was roundly criticized for its ineptitude in handling the resulting disaster. The poor performance of the agency under Brown's direction led to his resignation from the position.

But Brown was not the only appointee at fault. In the wake of Hurricanes Katrina and Rita, the federal government allowed political appointees to "filter scientific information before it reached the public, overriding the judgment of health officials" (Pope, 2006, p. 8). Combined with a lack of preparedness to offer assistance, and a willingness to "suspend health standards for toxic clean-ups", the ill-advised actions of political appointees contributed to the crisis (ibid).

Agency underperformance due to political appointees has been found in multiple academic studies. Consider a 2008 survey conducted by the National Academy of Public Administration (NAPA). This online instrument gathered answers from career employees of the Senior Executive Service (SES), an organization from which non-political appointees are often drawn.

A paper presented at the 2009 Midwestern Political Science Association's annual meeting used data from this survey to draw some disheartening conclusions about the effects of appointees on the federal government's functioning. Using PART scores, the study found that increased layering of political appointees leads to increased organizational dysfunction (Resh, 2009). This finding poked holes in a federal assumption about the benefits of political appointees; namely, that "since Reagan, increased layering of political appointees within federal agencies was thought to increase direct responsiveness to presidential prerogatives" (ibid). After all, responsiveness to White House directives matters little if the agency cannot function properly.

Public Disservice. 2005 was a bad time for political appointees as far as the weather was concerned, and it wasn't simply the fault of multiple hurricanes. Climate change also blew an ill wind for them—a wind some of them tried to hide by altering or withholding scientific data.

NASA's Inspector General issued a report that exposed how political appointees in its public affairs office from 2004–2006 "reduced, marginalized, or mischaracterized" data and scientific findings NASA had gathered on climate change (Hogue, 2008, p. 13). The Bush-administration appointees in this office "altered or withheld NASA press releases" about these findings, and "tried to stop James E. Hansen, director of the agency's Goddard Institute for Space Studies and its top climate scientist, from speaking to the news media" (ibid).

Disservice to the public by political appointees runs far deeper than obfuscating information about climate change. In the case of the Food and Drug Administration (FDA), disservice can be downright fatal. The FDA is responsible for issuing warning letters to companies whose products and related services are presenting documented public health hazards, and these letters are a "company's last chance to eliminate a hazard before being sued or having its product seized" (Zegart, 2006, p. 24). Under "Bush-appointed FDA chief counsel Dan Troy", the number of these agency letters sent out dropped "from 1,154" in the year 2000 to "535 in 2005", and "seizures of mislabeled, defective, or dangerous products... dipped 44 percent" (ibid).

What were Troy's qualifications for his position? Prior to the appointment, he had made a career of suing the FDA for corporate clients such as Brown & Williamson Tobacco "which successfully blocked the FDA's historic attempt to regulate cigarettes" (ibid). Troy's office proved its lack of concern for public health by ignoring a lower FDA district office's request to issue a warning letter to a blood bank which killed a patient by administering the wrong type of blood, a mistake the bank had made multiple times (ibid). While not as dramatic or nationally well-known as FEMA's incompetence during Katrina, the FDA's indifference is no less fatal.

Once Troy had served his term, he was replaced in 2005 by Sheldon Bradshaw, an appointee who had "no relevant experience with food or drug issues" (ibid, p. 28). And so it continues.

Ineffectiveness of Short Terms. Even a political appointee dedicated to good service and transparent access to information has a hard time carrying out these missions, for time is exactly what he lacks. "The average tenure of an appointee is 2.5 years", compared to an average chief executive tenure of five to seven years in the private sector (Pfiffner, 2012, p. 38). Political appointees serve for only a short time, and much of it is spent being confirmed for the job and being oriented to it. The remaining time may be equally unproductive as the administration which appointed him can be voted out of office, leaving him in the lurch. The short term also means that positions can become vacant before a president's term ends, and the vacancies lead to "agency inaction, uncertainty for civil servants in implementing programs, and lack of accountability" (ibid, p. 37).

Former Rear Admiral Stuart Platt detailed the difficulties he confronted due to short-term political appointees in his 2002 book, *The Armament Tide*. Platt focused on military acquisitions, an area overseen by the Under Secretary for Defense (Acquisition and Technology). To Platt, the short-term duration of an appointee's tenure is a major problem.

"An incoming Secretary or Under Secretary... usually will have the first months of his term taken up by confirmation hearings, additional months dedicated to being brought up to speed, and then a period of two years in which he can play an effective role, followed by a year in which he suffers as a lame duck if it appears the incumbent president will not be reelected." (Platt, 2003).

Platt's timeline for being brought up to speed may be overly optimistic. "Analysts widely agree that appointees need at least a year to become productive performers in their government posts" (Kettl, 2012, p. 292). Neither does he fully take into account the effect of that second year of service being an appointee's last. Faced with programs that take many years to implement and evaluate, and the reality that deep organizational change can require a timeline of five to seven years, the political appointee has a significant incentive to go for short-term goals (ibid). Achieving short-term gains can win public support for the appointee and the administration which appointed him, but the agency's long-term goals suffer in the meantime.

Those long-term goals get pushed aside for the next leader to handle, who will have just as strong an incentive to pass the buck to the next appointee after him. Careerists in these agencies can get pulled first one way and then the other, as a succession of appointees drag the agency this way and that in pursuit of short-term goals. This undoubtedly contributes to the frustration and morale problems many career administrators experience in the civil service.

Nowhere are these problems summarized as succinctly as in the Government Accountability Office's study of the Social Security Administration (SSA), where the GAO found the SSA had *seven* different commissioners from 1978 to 1987. The GAO had this to say: "These short tenures, along with commissioners' differing priorities and management approaches, resulted in frequent changes of direction, diminished accountability, and little long-term planning" (ibid, p. 293).

Rear Admiral Platt proposed longer terms as part of the solution, both to centralize defense acquisition and keep it from breaking down due to these political shifts and administration changes. Rather than lengthening the undersecretary's term, Platt's solution involves the creation of a new position: the Chief of Defense Materiel Procurement, who would serve a six-year term to "ensure continuity through changes in administrations" (ibid). Given the vacancy problems caused by confirmation delays on the front end, the vacancy problems caused on the back end when short terms are over, and the agency ineffectiveness caused in the middle, longer terms certainly seem like a reasonable solution.

But, as explored in the previous *Why Appointees* section, this solution ignores the shifting control political parties experience when Congress and the President come from two different parties. The short terms are valuable to Presidents precisely because they are short. When control of the presidency shifts from one party to another, that President will desire to "stock the pond" with appointees from his own party, not the opposing one. A six-year term would exceed the four-year term served by the President, virtually guaranteeing conflict and opposition in the cases where control flips to another party after that term.

Four-year terms would be the obvious suggestion here, but by the time the nomination and process are over, we have zero guarantee that the four years will exactly coincide with any given presidential term. The literature also suggests that the sheer number of appointees be reduced, but this solution would require cooperation between Congress and presidents which is nowhere to be found. Congress would need to convert the appointee positions into ones for career staff, but "presidents claim they need these positions to steer the administration" (Kettl, 2012, p. 295).

Until both the executive and the legislature can agree that the problems of political appointees are real, that their existence and proliferation subvert the goals of both branches and the public, and that fewer appointees serving longer terms is a viable solution, the problem will not go away. It will only get worse.

D. Contemporary Background.

Contemporarily, concerns about strategic human capital management have come to the forefront of the government's perspective on its labor force. Concerns about the performance of political appointees often merge into a larger problem of human capital in the literature, so they merit examination from this broad perspective.

The GAO and Political Appointees as Labor. The Office of Personnel Management, along with the Office of Management and Budget, has studied the federal workforce within the framework of strategic human capital management, and have created new performance measurement systems within this framework. But the federal leader in the realm of studying human capital is the GAO.

The U.S. Government Accountability Office (GAO) considers strategic human capital management as an area where the federal government is at high-risk, and it has offered general recommendations on how to mitigate this risk. For "federal agencies to change their cultures and... become high-performing organizations," they need to recruit and retain "a federal workforce able to create, sustain, and thrive in organizations that are flatter, results-oriented, and externally focused" (Goldenkoff, 2008, p. 1).

"The importance of a top-notch federal workforce cannot be overstated. The nation is facing new and more complex challenges in the 21st century as various forces are reshaping the United States and its place in the world. These forces include a large and growing long-term fiscal imbalance, evolving national and homeland security threats, increasing global interdependence, and a changing economy" (ibid).

In 2002, the GAO warned that "looming retirements in the next five years" could damage the Department of Housing and Urban Development's ability to "carry out its mission" (Lunney, 2007). Five years later, nearly 2,000 HUD employees were eligible to retire, many of them political appointees who were already "leaving the federal government at a fast clip" (ibid). Aside from the challenges of re-staffing positions held by career executives, this also presages a pile-up in the Senate, whose lengthy confirmation process and ensuing delays contribute to the problems of political appointees. "The civil service is aging," warns Walker, and "too few agencies have succession plans in place", leading to a dangerous lack of "people with the right skills and a sense of stewardship" to responsibly fill the vacant positions (Walker, 2007).

Futhermore, the retirements of career administrators cannot be considered a separate phenomenon from concerns about political appointees. Many administrators retire exactly *because* of poorly chosen appointees. Dan Troy's pro-corporate, anti-public reign at the FDA caused many administrators to give up and walk away in frustration at such blatant disregard for the agency's mission of protecting public health, an event echoed across the Environmental Protection Agency (EPA) and Department of Justice (DOJ), where careerists left in droves during the Bush administration.

The White House had "put people in charge of many offices who simply [didn't] believe in the mission of the office... And they are there to ensure that those offices will never return to carrying out the policies or enforcing the law", according to a veteran of the DOJ's civil rights division (Zegart, 2006, p. 24). The result? 20 percent of the division's litigators quit in fiscal year 2005 alone (ibid, p. 26). Other agencies fared little better. From 2000 to 2001, political appointees at the FDA carried out a "steady erosion of influence by the career staff", eventually rendering them "excluded and powerless in decision-making", according to the FDA's former associate commissioner William

Hubbard (ibid).

These disgruntled and disillusioned retirees carry with them valuable experience and institutional memory, signifying a great loss to the federal government's ability to serve the people. Combined with a tendency for political appointees to serve special interests rather than the general public, the retirements of career civil servants bode ill for our nation.

Evolving Attitudes of Political Appointees. But not every political appointee deserves to be cast in the villainous light which many deserve. Contemporary attitudes among political appointees can also show a great appreciation for the value career executives bring to civil service. For example, when appointee John Shaw became assistant secretary for environment, safety, and health at the U.S. Department of Energy, he told the press, "I'm fortunate to have a team of professional career civil servants. If you come in with the attitude of us versus them, you fail" (Lunney, 2005).

Shaw's positive attitude toward career administrators may have something to do with his prior experience in federal management, "something many political appointees lack," including his time as "deputy chief of staff to outgoing Energy Secretary Spencer Abraham" and serving as "the department's liaison to the White

House" (ibid). As deputy chief of staff, he was responsible for "implementing President Bush's five-point management agenda, which includes improving the recruitment and retention of the federal workforce" (ibid).

Shaw clearly understood the need for cooperation between political appointees and career executives, and the value of the latter to his department's mission. According to his LinkedIn profile, Shaw went on to senior executive positions in DC-based private and nonprofit companies after leaving the Department of Energy in 2006. Shaw stands out from other problematic appointees used as examples in this paper, a fact that suggests a certain amount of bias in media's reporting of the failures of such appointees.

See the *Limitations of Previous Research* section for more detail on this bias.

Evolving Policy about Political Appointees. Policy, too, has shifted regarding political appointees, especially where lobbyists are concerned. Lobbyists are problematic for the federal government because they are a double-edged sword. On the one hand, appointing them to agency positions runs the risk that the agency will fall under the undue influence of the very industries it was meant to regulate. For example, when Tom Wheeler became Chairman of the Federal Communications Commission (FCC), many feared that the nation's Internet policy would be under the control of the cable companies he had previously represented.

That these cable companies filed suit against the FCC following the issuance of the *2015 Open Internet Order* (more commonly known as "net neutrality") shows that Wheeler ended up opposing these same special interests. (For a more complete examination of this order, its history, and meaning, see my 2015 publication, *Net Neutrality for Broadband: Understanding the FCC's 2015 Open Internet Order*.)

Wheeler exemplifies the other edge of the lobbyist sword: Who has more specialized knowledge, experience, and contacts in the given field or industry than the lobbyists who mediated between Congress and these private companies? Where else would the federal system find people with the skills to manage these concerns for the nation, if not from within the private sector actually carrying out the operations and implementation of the field to be regulated?

The Obama administration understands this concern. After all, it was President Obama who nominated Wheeler in 2013. But the Obama administration has chosen not to handle the sword lightly. In his first week as President, Obama created new rules to "reduce the influence of lobbyists in policy decisions by barring former lobbyists from working for the administration on matters for which they lobbied during the previous two years" (Schouten, 2010, p. 7a).

But this policy was subject to a certain degree of flexibility. For example:

"Deputy Defense Secretary William Lynn and White House aides Jocelyn Frye and Cecilia Muñoz received broad waivers from rules that would have barred them from working on issues about which they lobbied or for the agencies they contacted as lobbyists. In those cases, White House officials said it was in the public interest to waive the rules because all three had vital experience" (ibid).

Finally, given the problems of delays in the Senate confirmation process, changes to the process of confirming appointees have evolved. For example, the 112th Congress passed S. 679 (The Presidential Appointment Efficiency and Streamlining Act of 2011) to reduce the number of executive positions requiring Senate confirmation (Pfiffner, 2012, p. 40). However, the reduction was not a substantial one, and it only addressed the confirmation process—not the number of political appointees in general, nor any of the other problems they so clearly create.

Evolving Powers of Political Appointees. Policy has also shifted regarding certain powers of political appointees. Given that agencies often create regulatory law (as opposed to the statutory law created by Congress), the power to veto said regulations would be a great power indeed, and the White House could exert no small amount of influence over agencies by granting political appointees this veto power. That's exactly what happened in 2007, when President Bush signed an executive order to allow "a political appointee in each agency to veto proposed regulations before they became public" (Nature, 2009, p. 775).

President Obama revoked this order concurrent with a request to Peter Orszag, then "head of the Office of Management and Budget (OMB), to suggest revisions to the office's fundamental principles for reviewing proposed government regulations" (ibid).

Rick Melberth, then head of regulatory policy at the Washington, DC group OMB Watch, was quoted as saying analysts there were "very happy" with this step at regulatory reform, that many of the problems predated the Bush administration, and that an increasing number of obstacles had, for three decades, been placed "in the way of agencies being able to regulate in a timely and effective manner" (ibid). It remains to be seen whether or not the next administration will uphold these measures or reverse the course by placing those obstacles once again.

E. Limitations of Previous Research. Prior research on the problems of political appointees and their effect on the federal labor workforce is, taken as a whole, fairly conclusive about both the nature of the problems, its causes, and its possible solutions. But the body of research is not without its limitations, such as a lack of data on certain key aspects of the problem, a tendency towards bias when using specific appointees as case studies, the self-reflexive problem of the federal government's attempts to study and repair itself, and tendency to focus on the problems as ones which performance measurement tools might solve rather than focusing on the social causes and effects of this ineffective system.

Lack of Data. While the Obama administration's more stringent restrictions on giving political appointments to lobbyists evidences a suspicion that lobbyists are potentially dangerous to the federal government's integrity, it is hard to say what hard facts contributed to it. Even simple data about the number of lobbyists is difficult to locate, because the government has not collected it. What data we do have comes from other groups who have researched the phenomenon in recent years.

A 2005 study "by the watchdog group Public Citizen found that more than 100 former lobbyists were appointed to government posts during

President George W. Bush's first term" (Schouten, 2010, p. 7a). The Obama administration worked to reduce this number by restricting the hiring of lobbyists, yet "two dozen employees out of nearly 2,900 high-level political appointees worked as registered lobbyists during the two years" prior to appointment by the administration (ibid). However, data is sorely lacking on this group, because "government agencies have not kept data on lobbyist hires in previous administrations" (ibid).

Biases in Reporting. In our examples of William Farish, Michael Brown, NASA public affairs office staff, Dan Troy, and others, the media may be biased in favor of finding fault with employees. Drawn to controversy by an "if it bleeds, it leads" philosophy, the so-called "news" outlets tend to focus on everything that's wrong. What about all the times a political appointee does a great job? Where are those stories?

The likely answer is that they are unreported. Even those who are openly critical of the government's performance must realize that we rarely hear about the times when government does its job exceedingly well. We are conditioned by controversy and make snap judgements based on headlines because we enjoy the intense emotional response and lack the time to dig deeper than the story on the surface and get the real facts. (See the case of the $600 hammers, which was simply wrong.)

Government Studying Itself. While one might convincingly argue that no one understands our sprawling federal government better than the government itself, we run the risk of having the foxes guard the hen house. Moreover, federal agencies which study this type of thing may be tied to the system by their vested interest in its continuation. Can an agency staffed by appointees truly have an interest in identifying and weeding out problems with appointees? Even if such an agency had no dirty laundry to air, it is likely to be networked with agencies that do.

It is also entirely possible that the government can't see into its own blind spots, much like authors are largely incapable of seeing their own bad habits or finding their own typos. The author's solution is to hire an outside editor and proofreader, and the government's solution may need a similar outside, disinterested party to identify its problems.

Focus on Performance. When the government does study itself, it chooses a particular framework that conceptually limits the problems. The human capital approach may well generate useful lessons and insights into the federal labor force, including political appointees, but the problems are more than just a human resources matter. Their far-reaching effects on society are rarely considered. Neither are the underlying causes built into the separation of powers system and its eternal bouncing back and forth between the control of only two parties like a massive bureaucratic ping pong ball.

And, by focusing on generally improving an agency's performance and employee management, the federal studies and assessment tools gloss over the specific problems of one type of staff member: the political appointee. To put the problem in perspective, a cancer patient visiting a family doctor needs more than to be told to eat right and exercise. Those are wonderful guidelines to general health, but they fail to address the cancer eating away at the patient from the inside.

Similarly, a broad focus on agency performance ignores the glaring problems with the political appointment system that clearly undermine agency performance. In other words, the OMB and the OPM can create all the performance measurement tools they want, but such tools are little use in rooting out the real—and very specific—problem which has plagued agencies for decades.

The literature agrees on the problems of political appointees, and it mostly agrees on the solutions: reducing the number of appointees, lengthening their terms, and opening current political appointee positions so that career executives and administrators can fill them instead. So, it makes little sense to continue to develop new performance assessment tools when the main cause of poor performance is already clear to researchers, and viable solutions to it are also known.

III. Implications of Current Findings.

When I first undertook a literature review on the limited question of the effects of short-term political appointments on society and the federal government, I doubted I would find sufficient material. My earliest sources amplified that doubt. For instance, Nina Mendelson's enlightening examination for Duke Law regarding the Senate's confirmation process clarified many of the negative effects of that cumbersome and constant endeavor. However, she reached a rather cavalier conclusion which amounted to, "It's really not that bad, so don't worry about it."

But the deeper I dug into the literature, the more I discovered just how real and pervasive the problems are, and how deeply they are woven into the structure of the federal government. I also found strong (though not entirely unanimous) agreement on the underlying causes, the negative effects, and the possible solutions. This widespread agreement is held by federal agencies dedicated to studying the executive branch labor force, along with academic researchers, former federal careerists, and even former appointees.

I also found agreement on why those solutions are not being put into place as part of a comprehensive reform to the system: the ongoing power struggle between the executive and the legislature, exacerbated by what is effectively a two-party political system in this country. So long as Republicans and Democrats continue to create an us-versus-them competition for control of the nation's policy-making process, presidents will retain an incentive to try wresting control of federal agencies and programs by staffing them with political allies, party members, campaign workers, and campaign contributors. Two bridges must be built: one between the executive and the legislature, and one between political parties. Only working in cooperation, not competition, can these forces unite to solve one of the federal government's most insidious problems.

At this stage in my research, I have reached the opinion that more research is not the key to solving these problems. The detrimental effects our current political appointee system has on the executive's ability to effectively serve the public are well-known, well-defined, and well-documented. The next step is not research but <u>action</u>.

A comprehensive reform bill would include several definite elements. The particulars may be up for discussion, but the general guidelines are crystal clear:

- Reduce the number of political appointees

in the executive workforce. This includes two prongs:

- o Reduce the number of layers of appointee positions, to decrease the burdensome thickening of executive management.
- o Convert many of these positions into ones which career administrators may fill instead of political appointees.

- Streamline the process by which the Senate confirms the executive's nominees, until that process can reach its historical duration of three months rather than averaging nearly a year.
- Increase the duration of the terms political appointees serve, so that they have time to not only get good at their jobs, but also take part in the long-term agency goals and deep organizational changes which require far longer than they currently have.

Taken together, these elements would do much to reduce the problems caused by vacant positions, and they would increase the morale of the career civil servants. They would create a federal culture where agencies could better use their human capital to become more effective instruments of public policy and public service.

The precise numbers of positions affected and the exact duration of the new terms are debatable questions, but the literature leaves little doubt about the importance of these elements. The most meaningful questions future researchers could ask are: How do we build a bipartisan coalition to draft, introduce, and advance this bill through the legislature? And, if that can be achieved, will we ever have a President who would sign it into law? What would it take to get Congress and the President to agree not only on the necessity of the reform, but on the actual policy measures needed to make it happen?

If the literature is any indication, the future is bleak for such a project, and the currently divisive political landscape of the United States does little to bolster our hopes for success. However, it is realistic to imagine that such a reform bill could at least be drafted by a person with the requisite legal experience; and if it can be drafted, it can be brought before the public to make people aware of the problem and begin to have a meaningful dialogue about its solution. This would be a project worthy of consideration for future work on this topic.

References

(February 12, 2009) "Obama demands rethink of regulatory processes." *Nature,* 457(7231): 775. doi:10.1038/457775a. http://palgrave.nature.com/news/2009/090211/full/457775a.html

Goldenkoff, Robert N. (May 8, 2008). *Human Capital: Transforming Federal Recruiting and Hiring Efforts,* GAO-08-762T, p. 1-17. "Testimony before the Subcommittee on Oversight of Government Management, the Federal Workforce, and the District of Columbia, Committee on Homeland Security and Governmental Affairs, US Senate." Prepared by the US Government Accountability Office. http://www.gao.gov/new.items/d08762t.pdf

Hogue, Cheryl. (June 9, 2008). "NASA Engaged In Spin: Agency political appointees downplayed climate-change data, inspector general's report says." *Chemical & Engineering News,* 86(23):13. http://cen.acs.org.ezproxy.fhsu.edu:2048/articles/86/i23/NASA-Engaged-Spin.html

Kettl, Donald F. (2012). *The Politics of the Administrative Process* (5ᵗʰ Edition). CQ Press (SAGE): USA. Chapter 9: *Human Capital*, p. 273-314.

Light, Paul C. (July 23, 2004). "Fact Sheet on the Continued Thickening of Government." *Brookings Institution.* https://www.brookings.edu/research/fact-sheet-on-the-continued-thickening-of-government/

Lloyd, Lorna. (2006). "Diplomats: A Breed Apart or Anyone Goes? The Question of Political Appointees as Heads of Mission." *Conference Papers–International Studies Association. 2006 Annual Meeting*, p. 1-16. http://citation.allacademic.com/meta/p_mla_apa_research_citation/0/9/9/3/1/pages99311/p99311-1.php

Lunney, Kellie. (January 22, 2005). "Around the Agencies." *National Journal,* 37(4): 228-230.

Lunney, Kellie. (April 14, 2007). "Vacancy Signs Sprout at HUD." *National Journal,* 39(15): 38.

Mendelson, Nina A. (May 2015). "The Uncertain Effects of Senate Confirmation Delays in the

Agencies." *Duke Law Journal,* 64(8): 1571-1606.

Nathanson, Philip. (Fall 2005). "Putting 'Strategic' in Human Capital Management." *Public Manager,* 34(3): 42-48. http://www.mcmanis-monsalve.com/files/publications/strategic-planning-fal-05-nathanson.pdf

Pfiffner, James P. (Winter 2012). "Strong Executive Branch Leadership Crucial for Policy Implementation." *Public Manager,* 41(4): 37-40.

Platt, Rear Admiral Stuart. (February 2003). "The Case for Transformation in Procurement." *U.S. Naval Institute Proceedings,* 129(2). (Edited excerpt from his book *The Armament Tide: Rearming America.* Granville Island, 2002.)

Pope, Carl. (Jan/Feb. 2006). "Disaster Denial." *Sierra,* 91(1): 8.

Resh, William. (2009). "Appointee Layering and Organizational Dysfunction: When Responsiveness is a Moot Point." *Conference Papers-Midwestern Political Science Association.* 2009 Annual Meeting. Abstract available at:

http://citation.allacademic.com/meta/p_mla_apa_research_citation/3/6/3/1/5/p363155_index.html

Schouten, Fredreka. (April 6, 2010). "Report reviews ex-lobbyists in top-level posts." *USA Today*. p. 7a.

Walker, David M. (Winter 2007). "GAO and Human Capital Reform: Leading by Example." *Public Personnel Management*, 36(4). https://www.questia.com/library/journal/1G1-174282948/gao-and-human-capital-reform-leading-by-example

Woodrow Wilson International Center for Scholars. (Summer 2013). "Heck of a Job, Appointee!" *Wilson Quarterly*, 37(3): 103-105. Article refers to the study: "The Consequences of Presidential Patronage for Federal Agency Performance" by Nick Gallo and David E. Lewis, in *Journal of Public Administration Research and Theory*, April 2012.

Zegart, Dan. (November 20, 2006). "The Gutting of the Civil Service." *Nation*, 283(17): 24-30.

www.ingramcontent.com/pod-product-compliance
Lightning Source LLC
Chambersburg PA
CBHW061737250726
48657CB00002B/972